Considering Conservation

Farming and Food Supply

Derrick Golland

Dryad Press Limited London

Contents

370778
JS

J. 338.19

ACKNOWLEDGMENTS

The author and publishers thank the following for their kind permission to reproduce copyright photographs: Melvin Almond/OXFAM, page 41 (bottom right); Heather Angel, page 18 (ladybird); Mark Boulton/International Centre for Conservation Education, page 8; Centre for World Development Education/World Bank, page 39 (bottom); CWDE/World Bank/K. Chernush, page 40 (top left); CWDE/World Bank/L. Daughters, page 25; CWDE/World Bank/Y. Hadar, pages 1, 6 (top left), 7 (right bottom), 15 (right), 20, 39 (top), 42; CWDE/World Bank/E. Huffman, pages 13 (right), 15 (left), 21 (top); CWDE/World Bank/I. Massar, page 11 (right); CWDE/World Bank/K. Muldoon, pages 9 (right), 41 (bottom left); CWDE/World Bank/R. Witlin, pages 10, 11 (left), 31 (left), 33 (bottom), 35 (right); Belinda Coote/OXFAM, page 3 (top); Farmer's Weekly, pages 6 (left centre), 12, 14, 17 (bottom), 22, 28 (left), 34, 36, 40 (bottom left), 43; Ana Cecilia Gonzales/OXFAM, page 29; Olivia Graham/OXFAM, page 23 (bottom); Greenpeace, page 37; Tony Gross/OXFAM, page 9 (left); Ross Hardy/OXFAM, page 17 (top); Jeremy Hartley/OXFAM, pages 31 (top), 35 (left); Brent Ingram, page 21 (bottom); Ministry of Agriculture, Fisheries and Food (Crown Copyright), page 41 (top left); OXFAM, page 6 (top right); Royal Agricultural Society of England, page 40 (bottom right); Sea Fish Industry Authority, pages 27, 38; War on Want, page 40 (top right). All other photographs are copyright of the author. The drawings on pages 8, 16, 20, 24, 30, 36 and on the cover are by R.F. Brien. The drawings on pages 27, 43 and 46 are by Sue Prince.

Cover illustrations

Top: CWDE/World Bank/R. Witlin
Centre: Farmer's Weekly (a stripper header)
Below left: Derrick Golland
Bottom right: R.F. Brien

Typeset by Tek-Art Ltd, Kent
and printed by
Anchor Brendon Ltd,
Tiptree, Essex
for the Publishers
Dryad Press Limited,
8 Cavendish Square,
London W1M 0AJ

ISBN 0 8521 9693 8

Why do people farm?

How do people obtain enough food to live? First they collect and hunt, but later, after realizing that if they *manipulate* nature, they can produce more food, more conveniently, they farm. A farmer may produce only enough food for his own family's needs, or he may produce more food than he requires, and so he can begin to trade. Trading brings the possibility of making a profit, and in a trading society the farmer, like any other businessman, is in business to make money.

Across the world, there is a sharp contrast between those who own nothing and produce little and those who, through land ownership and farming, make considerable profits.

There are many similar as well as contrasting ways in which Britain and developing nations use land for food production. Sometimes people use nature carefully, to their advantage. Sometimes they over-exploit it, with disastrous consequences. At present, British agriculture is beset by many problems which must be faced up to, since they affect every one of us and extend, through trade, far beyond the shores of our island. We have the opportunity to learn from our mistakes and assist developing nations in building a food production system that allows for sustainable development without destroying the earth's resources.

In this book you will be able to examine a number of farming and food supply topics in Britain and go on to relate them to global problems. As each page introduces you to new issues of farming and food supply, you must ask yourself: "Are the people involved *considering conservation*?"

Two faces of farming: a typical British farmer owning several hundred hectares of land and, in the Philippines, a poor woman planting food crops by the roadside.

Land values

Farming is big business; food is the major product, the land a farmer's chief resource.

In Britain, farmers either own their land, or they are tenants, renting all or a part of their farm from someone else. In both cases the value of the land plays a vital part in fixing the price of food. It is likely that a 10% rise in land value will eventually result in a 1% rise in the price of the product.

Let's look at the example of a tenant farmer. The owner of the land wants most of all to obtain a good income from his estates; he charges his tenant rent. The amount of the rent he charges is based partly on the suitability of the land for farming: a field of poor pasture, suitable only for rough grazing, is worth much less than a field of rich arable land which will yield plentiful crops for many years running. However, other factors, such as the availability of land, also affect the amount of rent charged. If there is a shortage of land, the value of what is available is greater; if there is more land available than there is a demand for, this lowers its value. So the amount of rent charged for the land may vary for economic reasons unconnected with farming.

The farmer has to respond to any changes in the rent. Usually he finds that he must pay increasingly high rents for the same land, and there is only one thing he can do: produce more, in an attempt to receive greater payments to meet his larger bills.

A rise in land values, passed on through his rent, may make the farmer buy more fertilizer to encourage crop growth, or use more pesticides to ensure better-quality crops. Another possibility is that he may increase his livestock numbers so much that there is a danger of their causing long-term damage to his grazing lands. This happens particularly with sheep on moorlands.

To maximize productivity, a farmer might examine the land in detail, identify all the unproductive areas and set out to make these useful. For example, filling in ponds, removing hedgerows and any field trees, and even reducing the amount of uncultivated land around gateways, are all ways of making extra

The majority of farmland in Britain is fertile and very valuable, thanks to many years of good husbandry.

Land is valued at a much higher price if it can be used for building rather than food production; here, close to the M6 in Staffordshire, new commuter homes will bear the names of a previous land-owner.

useful land out of areas which the farmer has been paying for, but which have brought him no financial return so far.

Almost certainly, an increase in the value of a farmer's land is bad news for the environment of the countryside. Changes of land use mean that wildlife habitats are lost, and water courses are polluted. The changes are necessary for both tenant farmers and owner-occupiers, whose livelihood is at stake, but this is a short-term problem compared with the environmental damage done. It is a difficult matter to consider, because whereas the value of land can easily be identified in terms of productivity, it is far harder to put a value on "environmental quality".

One solution, since the introduction of the Wildlife and Countryside Act in 1981, has been for the government to pay a farmer to *not* develop a wildlife habitat for agricultural purposes. The amount of compensation paid is still based on loss of likely agricultural output. One farmer, for example, receives £10,000 per annum to *not* run free-range pigs on heathland designated as a National Nature Reserve. A second is given at least £24,000 each year for agreeing to *not* turn a Dorset wood into fields of cereals or a plantation of coniferous trees.

In many respects, what has happened in Britain is a small version of the global problem.

Currently, many farms are being amalgamated to form bigger units. The old, traditional-style farm buildings and the land on which they stand suddenly become highly valued.

The individual farmer trying to make ends meet is like the developing nation facing a mountain of rising debts. Both need to increase their income from their resources. But is economic gain more important than conserving natural habitats? Society is built on an economic base, but, on the other hand, it can only survive in a natural world.

Conservation – who cares?

Agricultural methods can be much improved without adopting the use of big machines. The plough here, in Brazil, is modern, but the water buffalo does not need imported fuel and will not damage the soil. ▲

A store full of barley. Farmers try to produce as large ▲ a harvest as possible and so it is very easy to over-produce and be left with a surplus of crops. This causes the prices to fall. Should we farm less land?

These fishermen of northeast Brazil have responded to the heavy industrial pollution of their rivers by rearing pollution-resistant fish – Tilapia. ▼

Lime is lost through cropping the land. To prevent the soil from turning acid and less fertile, lime should be added. However, unlike the farmer here, many will try to avoid liming. This is false economy. ▼

◄ Ploughing immediately after the harvest leaves the land bare in the following months of heavy rain and much more subject to erosion.

◄ *Farming in Britain relies on a plentiful supply of good-quality water such as this stream gushing from a Welsh mountainside. But will it remain unpolluted on its route to the sea?*

In 1986 the sheep of North Wales and Cumbria could ➤ not be sold for food as they had been contaminated by radiation from a nuclear plant in the USSR.

The sea is the source of many people's food and yet we make limited attempts to manage it, and regularly use it as a dumping ground for our wastes. ▼

If farming is to be more profitable, its efficiency must be improved. The key to this often lies in building a good road network, but many habitats are destroyed in the process; in this case in Nigeria. ➤

Tree loss

Individual trees are constantly dying; it is part of the natural cycle. However, periodically, we suffer from large-scale tree loss that could perhaps have been prevented. True, the storm of October 1987 that destroyed so many trees in south-eastern England was a natural occurrence, but how many of the trees which fell in those high winds had, in fact, been weakened by a population that showed little care for them? Damage encourages disease; disease speeds death. Whilst most infection of trees is fairly localized there are sometimes countrywide, and even worldwide cases.

For instance, Britain's elm trees have suffered from many attacks of Dutch elm disease over the centuries. This is caused by a parasitic fungus, spread by a beetle, and usually results in the death of the tree. The latest outbreak of the disease began in 1967 and spread rapidly across the country. It was probably introduced in a consignment of timber from the USA, for making furniture veneer.

In 1979 it was estimated that 1 in 8 of the world's population of elm trees was dying each year. In Britain, the elm used to be a common hedgerow tree. There was a great public outcry as the disease devastated the elm population. Unsafe, diseased trees had to be felled, and today all that remains are stumps in the

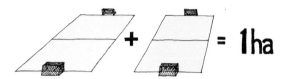

One hectare = the size of two football pitches.

hedgerows. The disease has therefore transformed the look of the landscape, and its ecology.

For farmers, the disease caused special problems. They lost many valuable timber trees, which they would eventually have sold to furniture makers. Countless hours that should have been spent in farming were spent felling unsafe trees that could then be sold for little more than the price of firewood. And the loss of elm trees led to a decline in the population of rooks, which normally lived in large colonies in tall elms, and scavenged the fields, helping farmers by ridding crops of insect pests.

It has been suggested that to ensure the growth of one new tree to maturity, at least eight must be planted. In other words, for each dead elm, eight new trees must be planted if we are simply to return our tree population to its former level.

It is ironic that the major outbreak of Dutch elm disease in 1967 should have stemmed from the importing of timber. Britain imports 90% of its timber needs, at a cost of well over £4,500 million each year. Whereas 30% of the world's land surface is covered in trees, this figure is only 9% for Britain, making it one of the least wooded countries in the European Economic Community (EEC). In West Germany, for example, 29% of the land area is covered in trees and the general public has legal right of access to all woodland. Clearing forests is

In Britain large areas of woodland have been destroyed to make way for farmland, but currently most losses are due to housing and new roads. Here oak woodland in Worcestershire is being removed.

illegal, and any felling that does take place must be accompanied by a replanting scheme.

In the case of Dutch elm disease, farmers were the victims of the tree loss, but in other cases, the blame can be placed fairly and squarely on their shoulders. Large areas of ancient, semi-natural woodland have been cleared, frequently to obtain more land for farming and often with government encouragement. In Northamptonshire, for example, the Nature Conservancy Council estimates that 694 hectares of important woodland have been destroyed in the last 50 years; in Gwent and Essex that figure approaches 1000 hectares.

Now, however, the farming community has too much land producing too much food (see pages 34-35). Many believe that the way ahead lies in "farm forestry", where large areas of farmland could be transferred to timber growing. Which trees might the farmer plant? He could select native British species such as oak, ash or beech; these would provide a valuable habitat for British wildlife. Or he could choose quicker-growing imported species such as conifers.

The loss of trees in Britain, though great, is insignificant by comparison with the destruction of the world's tropical rainforests. The rainforests are some of the most species-rich areas of land in the world and therefore they are vital genetic reserves (see page 21), but they are disappearing at a rate of 11 million hectares a year, at the hands of agriculturalists, timber merchants and fuel-wood gatherers. Such extensive clearances lead to major changes in

The market place of Harar, Ethiopia, is a gathering place for fuel-wood collectors who hope to make a little extra money by selling their load.

Destroying these Brazilian forests by felling and fire is a quick means of obtaining extra agricultural land in the short term; ultimately it could spell disaster for the world.

the local climate; there is frequently a reduction in rainfall, and the rain now comes in the form of a tropical downpour and rapidly washes away the soil since this is devoid of vegetation. The land thus becomes useless for growing any food and a hostile environment for wildlife. The balance of the climate worldwide is also affected by the vast destruction of the forests. Temperature and rainfall are altered.

The United Nations Food and Agriculture Organization estimates that 2 thousand million people depend on wood as their primary source of energy; of these, 96 million cannot find enough timber even to supply their minimum needs.

In Central Sudan, gum-arabic trees have formed an important part of the crop rotation. However, the fuel needs of the people are so great that farmers found that they could chop down the trees, convert them to charcoal and sell this, and so increase their income by some 200%. Their gain was short-term. Now there is an acute shortage of fuel-wood and people must walk many miles in search of fresh supplies. Some villagers may spend most of the year just gathering fuel. In an effort to replace some of the tree cover in Sudan, Oxfam has established a community forest project.

Expensive labour

In 1951 a lowland Staffordshire dairy farm of 170 hectares employed thirteen men. By 1958 that number had fallen to seven, and today the same farm employs only two men. It is surprising, therefore, to learn that the farm produces more than it did nearly forty years ago. This is a pattern of change repeated throughout much of lowland Britain.

There are three possible explanations for the reduction in labour. Firstly, as farmers continue to strive for greater overall economy in their business, farming has become more streamlined and less diversified – that is, the range of crops or animals on any one farm is much smaller. With less variety of jobs to be completed, fewer workers are needed. Secondly, a general farm worker can expect to earn a good living wage each week. Therefore, if the farmer can dispense with just one employee, he can make considerable savings in the course of a year. Thirdly, scientific developments and technological advancements have brought about the disappearance of time-consuming jobs where "many hands made light work".

As recently as fifty years ago, a farmer's major capital investment (his money) was in his land. Today, however, he spends an increasing amount of his financial resources (often borrowed) on sophisticated equipment and machinery, or on chemicals. Money spent on these means he can avoid several labour-intensive, time-consuming processes. Today, grass can be killed off with chemicals rather than ploughed in; seeds can be drilled directly into uncultivated soil; or crops such as potatoes can be sprayed from the air to prepare them for harvest.

Harvesting a cereal crop illustrates well how the British farmer has used improved technology, and become more efficient, while reducing the size of his labour force. In post-war Britain the mechanical reaper was still common. This produced sheaves of corn that had to be stood up, by hand, in groups of three or four. The bundles of sheaves were known as stooks. They then had to be transported to the farmyard and fed through the threshing machine to separate grain from straw – the former to be bagged, the latter baled and stacked. A team of 10-15 workers was needed for this. Today, a combine harvester driven by one man can do the bulk of the work. Only two

Throughout the developing world farming and food production is the responsibility of women. These women in Senegal are preparing the ground for planting with rice.

or three other drivers are needed to cart away the grain and bale the straw if it is to be saved (see page 24).

To work efficiently, sophisticated machinery like the combine harvester requires a weed-free crop that grows to a standard height. Therefore, new varieties of plant are developed to meet the needs of the machine, and plants previously thought of as "wild flowers" are eradicated by several quick actions of weedkiller. In encouraging methods which reduce labour – and, consequently, the wage bill – the farmer reshapes the countryside.

In other parts of the world, the agricultural labour force is very different. In Indonesia, for example, the number of people involved in food production is estimated to be as high as 80% of the 160 million population. In most developing countries it is the women who grow more than

These six men stacking sheaves of wheat in Ethiopia are reminiscent of a bygone age in Britain.

half of the food produced, and they are responsible for processing an even larger share. Seventy per cent of food crops in sub-Saharan Africa are grown by women.

It is often part of the culture of the people for the woman to be the provider of food while the man remains the figurehead of the family. Also, today, many males have become migrant workers, heading off to seek their earnings in larger towns or cities, or acting as the labour force in the harvesting of cash crops on large plantations. This again leaves the women at home to produce the food.

In African countries, the initial clearing and ploughing of land is traditionally a male occupation. Aid from Western nations has frequently been used to provide tractors and improved equipment and these have enabled the men to clear greater areas of land more efficiently. The women, however, are left to plant, weed, harvest and generally care for the larger areas of crops, using the same methods as before. Their tools are usually little more than a hoe and a sickle. To improve farming methods, agricultural education is essential, but the United Nations Development Programme has noted that courses are attended mainly by men – not by the women who do the work! Consequently, improvements are hard to bring about.

Tea pickers at work on a tea plantation in Kenya; traditionally a very poorly paid job.

11

The rise of the big machine

Early in the 1860s Mr Smith of Woolston, Buckinghamshire, was able to proclaim that his was "the first whole farm ever tilled by a steam engine". However, as steam-powered engines were, by and large, too heavy to move across the fields, their use was confined to pulling a plough across a field by means of a hawser (steel rope), or to powering the threshing machines. In 1902 Dan Albone produced the first British tractor and by 1920 farmers had purchased around 10,000 machines. Demand was so great that most of these, in fact, had to be imported from America, where the first tractor with an internal combustion engine had been built in 1889. Nevertheless, British farmers continued to rely on horse-power for several decades and as recently as in 1950, 300,000 horses were still at work on British farms.

Today, when we look back, horse-power often seems attractive; but it had many disadvantages. The animals had to be fed and groomed before and after work, and this often extended the working day by four or five hours. The animals' work-rate was slow and it would take a horse about 2½ days to plough one hectare, during which time the horse and ploughman would have walked over 27 miles (43 km). Even if a farmer had a large team of horses, their pulling power limited the size and type of equipment that could be used and prevented any deep ploughing. Moreover, the fuel requirements of this living source of motive power were considerable. A working horse would have to be fed around 7 kg of oats and beans each day. These had to be grown on the farm, using up land that might otherwise have been planted with food crops that could have been sold to the ever-increasing urban population.

In a few decades the tractor has developed into a sophisticated machine, complete with air-conditioned cab and a stereo radio. It costs upwards of £15,000. In contrast to the ploughman, whose feet were firmly in contact with the ground, the tractor driver is almost completely insulated from the outside world.

In 1985 British farmers purchased 25,000 new tractors. Compared with other European farmers they prefer bigger-powered models and, although the average tractor engine size is 61kW, over 1000 vehicles powered at over 90kW are sold to British farmers annually. One of the largest models currently in use has a

There are only a few British farmers who can justify buying a tractor as large as this one.

A combine harvester can be operated by one man, and yet carries out the work of several different machines.

In many parts of the world farmland is still cultivated using oxen. This farmer is at work high in the Andes mountains of Ecuador.

243kW engine, weighs over 12 tonnes and has a tank that can hold more than 1,000 litres (222 gallons) of fuel. For an explanation of tractor engine size, see **tractor power** in the Glossary.

Farmers see these large machines as a way to become more efficient. By using a large tractor, they are able to reduce the number of workers employed and carry out cultivation and harvesting tasks at a much greater speed. However, to justify the cost of buying such a machine, the farmer needs to keep it working for as many hours as possible and so the working day is extended to 20 hours. During this time such a tractor will be able to cultivate 40 hectares of land. It will consume 40 litres of fuel per hour, or 20 litres per hectare, and cost in the region of £25 per hectare to run.

To the farmer, or agricultural contractor who hires out his services, these machines represent a major investment. However, the much sought-after efficiency can only be achieved if the landscape is altered to suit the big machines. Any field obstacles, such as hedgerows or trees, must be eliminated. And so the cost of efficiency is much more than just the £70,000 paid for the tractor.

The British farmer's pursuit of super-efficiency may be coming to an end, however. If mounting surpluses of food can be reduced only by the farmer producing less, then one answer may be for him to be less intensive in his methods. In that case, the purchase of the "big machine" may become a thing of the past.

As a nation of tractor drivers, Britain is in sharp contrast to other parts of the world. In India, for example, there are estimated to be some 80 million draught animals still at work. This represents a power output equivalent to 30,000 megawatts. (A megawatt is a million watts.) Compare this with the sales of new tractors in Britain in 1985 which, in total, had a power output of 1,527,247kW! In southern Sudan, when agriculturalists talk of a much-needed technological revolution, they mean the introduction of the plough and bullock to do work currently done by hand and hoe!

There is a great danger that as tractor sales slump in Europe and the USA, manufacturers will try to sell them instead to the developing nations. They may well be tempted to promote there a product that is wholly inappropriate to the needs of both the society and the environment.

Chemical fertilizers

The vast majority of crops rely on a regular supply of nutrients from the soil to maintain adequate growth. Farmers have realized that by changing and controlling the basic chemistry of the soil, they can control the growth rate of the plant and its eventual yield.

Soil has six main elements, and several others in small quantities, but three elements have been identified as the most important. Nitrogen encourages rapid growth; Phosphorous – essential to all living cells – ensures the development of a strong stem and root system; and Potassium is vital for the control of carbon dioxide in photosynthesis. A farmer will frequently apply all three of these chemicals at once, although in differing ratios according to the crop. When the three chemicals are applied together, they are known as a "compound fertilizer".

The use of chemical fertilizers has risen by eight times since 1950 and is very much a trend of the second half of the twentieth century. Before 1950, farmers relied extensively on nitrates imported from Chile, sulphate of ammonia which was available as a by-product of the manufacture of coal gas, and superphosphates. Superphosphates were derived from bone-meal (ground-up animal bones) treated with sulphuric acid. Organic fertilizers in the form of horse and cow manure were also used extensively.

Unlike manure, chemical fertilizers are the product of an industrial process. To gain some idea of the effect they have had on farming, we need only compare different yields. In the twelfth century Britain's average corn yields are estimated to have been only about 350 kilogrammes per hectare, largely because of the shortage of nitrates in the soil, but also because of inferior crop varieties. Today it is possible to grow 15-16 tonnes of wheat per hectare, although only as a result of applying fertilizer dressings of as much as 1,500 kg (1.5 tonnes) per hectare per year.

Substantial amounts of fertilizer are needed to maintain the national average of over 6 tonnes of wheat per hectare. One of the most worrying aspects of modern farming is the ill-treatment of the soil this represents. Cropping

Today, British farming relies heavily on the use of chemical fertilizers. Nitrates in particular may not be fully used up and quickly leave the soil and enter unseen water courses; their presence in streams and rivers has to be carefully controlled if they are not to be a danger.

the same land year after year for corn, and continuously applying chemical fertilizers, reduces the natural fertility of the soil. Eventually, the fields are so infertile that they can only grow crops with the aid of the chemicals. The soil becomes weakened so that it is prone to erosion by wind and water, and so a natural resource is lost (see also Soil conservation, page 22). Once he has established the habit of applying large quantities of fertilizer to the land, it is almost impossible for

14

the farmer to stop, because of his fear that his land will then cease to yield as much. Farmers are frequently guilty of employing a "play safe" policy when applying fertilizer. They put on as much as they can afford, which is invariably far too much.

Any nitrogen from the fertilizer which is not taken up by the crop or incorporated into the soil's organic matter is lost. In spring, especially, the nitrogen is converted into a gas which is released into the atmosphere in a process called *denitrification*. In wet weather, nitrogen not taken up by the plants is washed down below the root zone and gradually out of the soil, polluting streams, rivers and other sources of water; this is known as *leaching*. It has been estimated that one third of the money spent on nitrogen fertilizers by British farmers is wasted in one of these ways.

On the other hand, fertilizer is scattered directly into the water of the paddy fields in the Philippines.

Chemical fertilizers today are very costly, largely because their manufacture relies on an industrial process fired by expensive fossil fuels. The price of these fuels has soared in recent years and so, in consequence, has the price of the fertilizer.

Agricultural scientists have developed many new high-yielding strains of crops to cope with the increasing demand for food worldwide. Sometimes this development is referred to as the "green revolution". Invariably, the new strains of crops have been "high-response"

varieties of plants which, when given a much greater supply of fertilizer than usual, produce an abnormally high yield.

For example, a developing nation might only apply 25 kg of nitrogen per hectare. If this amount is increased, say, by about three times, to 70-90 kg per hectare, the yield is multiplied by many more times than three. The farmer becomes trapped into paying increased prices for fertilizer, in order to remain in business, and the nation as a whole must attempt to buy fertilizer, whatever the price, in order to maintain the supply of food to its people.

There are alternatives. We rely on only a very small number of plant species to provide us with food. If botanists can identify a wider range of food plants, particularly those already growing in a specific area and needing no major artificial inputs for a good crop, then we might begin to meet the worldwide demand for food. Also, if scientists teach farmers to make greater use of soil biology, ensuring the development of both animals and soil features that enhance fertility, then many farmers may be able to escape from the habit of using more and more chemicals and produce more food at a lower cost.

Distributing fertilizer in Nigeria. Many developing nations are being encouraged to expand their use of fertilizer rapidly. Is this a good idea?

Pesticides

As you select your purchases from the supermarket shelf, or sit down to enjoy your Sunday lunch, you probably take for granted the quality of the food before you, and so you almost certainly overlook the vital role that pesticides have to play in everyday life.

Pesticides include insecticides and herbicides. They are substances, or products, designed to control the undesirable effects on crops of either animal or vegetable pests. A herbicide controls weeds in a crop and prevents them from using the soil nutrients which the crop needs. An insecticide controls, and usually kills, insects which may feed off crops or carry disease to livestock. Pesticides thus improve the quality, yield and appearance of the crops.

In Britain, pesticides have contributed to an overall 2% annual increase in yields in recent decades. In contrast, it is estimated that most Third World nations lose at least one third of their crops to pests. The British Agrochemicals

Large pesticide sprayers such as this are a common feature of British farms.

Association estimates that, if we did not use pesticides, "the United Kingdom cereal yields would drop by about 25% in the first year, and 45% in the second".

Chemical pesticides are not a new idea. One thousand years ago the Chinese were using arsenic to control garden insects. In the last fifty years, however, there have been rapid advances.

INSECTICIDES

Insecticides can be identified in three main groups – organochlorines, organophosphates and pyrethroids. The organochlorines were introduced in the early 1940s, and the most well-known kinds were DDT, Aldrin and Dieldrin. The last two were used as seed-dressing (seeds are coated with a chemical to ward off any pests) until the early 1960s, when it was realized that, like DDT, these chemicals become increasingly concentrated as they move up the food chain, until they eventually reach lethal amounts in predators such as sparrowhawks and peregrine falcons. In certain cases, bird populations were almost wiped out.

Organochlorines persist in the environment (they do not break down like other chemicals)

Follow the pesticide route through this food chain: thistle – slug – thrush – hawk.

for many years and this, along with their ability to stick to dust particles and to evaporate with water into the atmosphere, as part of the rain cycle, makes them extremely dangerous. Nevertheless, in the Third World, despite the many dangers to humans and wildlife, DDT is still used in the control of malaria-bearing mosquitoes and also as a general insecticide. It is banned in the USA, although produced in large quantities there, and in Britain its use is strictly limited. However, it can still find its way into our diet on imported foods.

This group of insecticides is being replaced by the organophosphates (descendants of wartime nerve gas such as Malathion are used to replace DDT) and the pyrethroids. The latter have a big advantage since they break down quickly after application and are much less poisonous for any mammals that may come into contact with them.

In developing nations farm workers often pay little attention to the hazards of pesticides, even when trained to use modern equipment. This man is spraying locusts in eastern Sudan.

HERBICIDES
Chemicals to control weeds – herbicides – have a more recent history, beginning in 1896 with the use of copper sulphate in France. By 1930 the French were spraying 200,000 hectares of cereals each year with diluted sulphuric acid! In Britain it is sometimes still used on potatoes. Herbicides have developed rapidly in both range and application. Today, some 44% of the amount spent by the world on agricultural chemicals is spent on herbicides; 33% is spent on insecticides.

Pesticides are highly toxic and can seriously affect the health of the person who is applying them. British law requires the worker to be well protected.

Herbicides are used in other complex ways, as well as just as total weedkillers. Paraquat, for example, which is very useful for disposing of weeds around the farmyard or the field boundary, is frequently used to speed up farming operations. When sprayed on to old grassland, its effects show in a few hours. After several days the grass is dead and the farmer can drill seed directly into the earth without ploughing the land beforehand. This method is increasingly used in the sowing of fodder crops such as swedes, turnips and kale. Once the seed has germinated and begun to grow, a "selective" herbicide such as clopyralid will kill weeds without harming the crop. Different mixes of chemicals are available depending on the crop and the particular weeds to be controlled.

COST AND COMPLEXITY
It may cost an agricultural company up to £30 million to develop one product and it must recoup this through sales. Pesticides are expensive and many developing nations are too poor to afford adequate supplies. A highly sophisticated product demands complex and expensive methods of application and requires the user to have considerable knowledge and experience. However, the person responsible for applying these highly toxic chemicals is often the semi-literate peasant farmer, who is unable to read the complex instructions, never mind afford the necessary protective clothing.

Biological controls – predators and pollinators

Farming is *unnatural* in that it involves trying to direct the world of nature to meet human needs and so inevitably upsets the natural balance. For example, to grow a particular crop most efficiently, the farmer must keep at bay other species which are usually found in the area; this is one reason why the use of herbicides has become so important (see pages 16-17). At the same time, the concentration of a particular crop in a given area may well lead to a population explosion of the insects that use the crop plant as a source of food.

Nature employs its own controls and it is reasonable to assume that these can be identified by scientists and used by farmers to their advantage. Protecting crops using natural methods is known as "biological control". Across the world, nearly 100 species of weed have been identified for biological control and, currently, successful techniques have been developed for about 25 per cent of them.

Perhaps the most outstanding example of biological control is the use of a species of moth to destroy the Prickly Pear in Australia. The Prickly Pear is a cactus native to Mexico. It was introduced in Australia and by 1925 it occupied 25 million hectares and was spreading at the rate of 400,000 hectares each year, creating impenetrable thickets which made the land useless for grazing or cultivation. Then a species of moth, *Cactoblastis cactorum*, was deliberately introduced from Argentina and within six years most of the cacti had been destroyed.

Growing crops in greenhouses is one of the most intensive methods of food production, but the carefully controlled environment of the greenhouse does much to encourage its own range of pests, one of which is the Whitefly. If you shake a plant which is infected by Whitefly, it will release clouds of these tiny insects; they will fly around for a while and then return to the underside of the leaves. They are commonly found on many greenhouse plants, but are a particular nuisance to tomato and cucumber growers. Whitefly feed off the plant and excrete "honeydew" on to the fruit, leaving the crop sticky. This limits growth and encourages the formation of moulds.

Whitefly can be controlled by introducing a minute parasitic wasp, *Encarsia formosa*. The wasps lay eggs in the Whitefly larvae, killing them, but ensuring a new generation of wasps. Eventually the wasps run out of larvae on which to breed. The Whitefly pest has been eliminated, and the wasps, too, now die out.

A major problem for many of Britain's farmers is the spread of bracken, a highly poisonous plant. It is resistant to most herbicides and its rhizomes spread rapidly through the ground, sending up shoots which open into large fronds and obliterate the

In early summer cereal crops are attacked by aphids. These will be naturally controlled, in part, by ladybirds.

Here you can see the Prickly Pear cactus spreading through scrubland in Tunisia. In that country it is used as a hedge-like barrier to keep out wandering livestock. Villagers have found, too, that they can harvest its fruit to sell in local markets.

grassland beneath. Currently, scientists are working on the possibility of introducing a moth from South Africa, *Conservula cinisigna*, the larvae of which can control the growth of bracken by tunnelling into the stems. First of all, however, scientists must be certain that the moth will not develop into a pest itself or be harmful to other existing species of plant or animal.

One problem is that the continued, often excessive, use of pesticides has not only got rid of the particular pest that the farmer wanted to kill but also limited the spread of a wide range of other species. This means that in controlling pests with pesticide, the farmer has frequently damaged the natural controls which were available to him.

A similar problem is that a general insecticide applied to destroy pests also destroys bees, which are an essential help for the farmer. The growth of many crops relies on pollination by bees, and farmers notice decreased yields, and therefore reduced income, as a result of a lack of bees. In 1980, scientists in America estimated that their pollination losses due to pesticides were at least £34 million per year. If the costs of reduced pollination are added to other assessed environmental costs of pesticides, the annual loss appears to have been in the region of £58 million. In parts of Tanzania and Kenya, where cotton is grown, the use of insecticide has almost completely put an end to beekeeping.

The developed nations have much for which to thank pesticides, even though their use has caused many problems. However, today we know that insects in particular can build up a resistance to pesticides and this means that new, more powerful chemicals must always be developed. In the light of our own experience, should we be seeking to develop biological controls that are appropriate to the developing nations so that they do not become as dependent on chemical pesticides as we are? To do this would require a much greater understanding of the natural environment and careful identification of the role of each of the species that might be beneficial to the farmer.

In the meantime, a new, potentially greater threat to the environment has loomed on the horizon. Scientists have been experimenting with introducing viruses as a form of biological pest control. How can a small group of people fairly work out all the possible results of using something as sinister as a virus? Can they be certain of keeping it under control, so that it will attack only those life-forms for which it is intended? Trials were abandoned in the USA, but are now taking place in Britain.

Encarsia formosa pupae are attached to a card which is mailed to the grower. Shortly after the card has been fixed to the plant, the pupae will hatch and begin to attack Whitefly, a common pest in greenhouses.

Genetic diversity

Life on earth is divided into five kingdoms – bacteria, single-celled organisms, fungi, plants and animals. Within each group there are millions of unique species that reproduce by one means or another and pass on their essential characteristics from one generation to the next via their genes. All living organisms are constructed from cells, and genes are transmitted as part of the chromosomes found in the nucleus of each cell.

When a species becomes extinct, a unique set of genes disappears. At the time, that loss may seem insignificant, but maybe, in the future, the characteristics of that lost species will prove vital.

There are some 145 indigenous breeds of cattle in Europe and the Mediterranean region, and this vast storehouse of differing characteristics helps the breeder maintain healthy varieties of livestock. However, all but 30 of these breeds are threatened with extinction, as farmers continue to breed only those animals that are best suited to their present needs. Current trends might well result in the European farmer becoming reliant on just one or two breeds. If these animals became susceptible to pests and diseases and we had lost the supply of varied genes from other breeds,

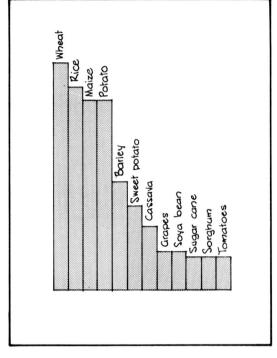

The top twelve crops worldwide (by tonnage).

Seed is often too expensive for poor communities to purchase. One means of providing extra supplies, and varieties, of crop is to establish a seed multiplication farm. Here in Gusau in Nigeria groundnuts are being planted.

then our food supply could be seriously threatened.

In the plant kingdom, the loss of genetic diversity is already critical. Man has learnt to use about 3000 species of plants for food, but trades in only 150 to any extent. Today, the vast majority of people rely on no more than 15 different plant species for their food supply. Placed in order of crop tonnage, the top five food-producing species are wheat, rice, maize, potato and barley.

Agricultural scientists are able to vary gene combinations to produce different varieties within a species (see also pages 14-15, Chemical fertilizers). They select parent plants, or animals, with suitable characteristics and combine them to produce a variety of plant or animal more able to overcome the problems encountered in the intended environment. Plants developed in this way give higher yields, grow more quickly, and have greater resistance to disease. They are easier to harvest, for example, producing shorter stalks or fewer leaves, and they have the ability to grow in hostile conditions. Each of these special qualities is important to the farmer.

When scientists develop a new variety of wheat, or other cereal crop, for growing in Europe or North America, they know that, within 15 years at the very most, the plants will succumb to pests and diseases, for these produce modified strains to attack the new crop. Extra pesticides then needed raise the cost of growing the crop, which may already be showing signs of a reduction in yield. As a result, the farmers' profits are lowered. This, coupled with constantly changing consumer demand, means that new crop varieties must regularly be introduced. To develop new varieties, scientists need a healthy genetic base from which to draw new materials.

The fact that most people in the Western world rely on a food supply from a domesticated or cultivated source does not mean that we can ignore the wild species (see also pages 36-37, Food from wildlife). It is the wild species that provide the essential genetic base, as well as offering an alternative to present food supplies. For example, to ensure that sugar-cane grown in the Indian sub-continent is resistant to the disease Red Rot, all cultivars (cultivated varieties) have been bred from a wild variety found in Indonesia and southern India. Wild maize found in Mexico has enabled the development of corn species resistant to Streak Virus, Africa's most serious disease affecting corn. Most of the resistance to the four main rice pests and diseases was bred into the Asian rice crop from a single wild rice found in central India.

Scientists agree that there are three ways of preserving genetic diversity. Firstly, we should protect the natural environment (the ecosystem) in which a species occurs, and of which it is an integral part. Secondly, we should establish gene banks in which seeds from plants, or semen from animals, can be stored until they are needed. Thirdly, organisms can be preserved in an artificial environment, such as a zoo or botanical garden, to be returned safely to their ecosystem as soon as possible. This third and often essential method is the least desirable, as a creature kept in a zoo, for instance, may modify its characteristics and so become not truly representative of the species in the wild.

A scientist at the International Rice Research Institute in the Philippines works on the development of new strains of rice.

All of these measures require detailed planning, which to many people may not seem worthwhile. However, surely their value is obvious if you think of the effects of a major catastrophe such as the radiation leak from Chernobyl in 1986. It may well be that the nuclear fallout will have long-term effects on the reindeer of Lapland, upsetting their ability to reproduce so that the species has only a limited chance of survival. All forms of genetic preservation must be necessary.

Wild pearl millet growing in Mali. Plant breeders are using this to improve varieties of pearl millet – a major cereal crop in the Sahel and northwestern India.

Soil conservation

Larger tractors mean heavier tractors! Inevitably soil structure is more likely to be damaged by compaction. Why do you think the farmer has fitted extra wheels to this tractor?

Early man noticed that seeds would often germinate more readily in disturbed soil than on bare, compacted earth. Using primitive tools such as sticks, antlers or stones, he began to loosen the soil himself. This was the beginning of cultivation. Today, for Western farmers, the cultivation of a seed bed is a highly complex process involving very specialized machines.

The plough, first known in England about 5,000 years ago, is still central to this activity. Ploughing loosens a heavy soil (which can then be broken down further by wind, rain and frost) and buries any existing plant material, such as remains of an earlier crop or natural vegetation. As he ploughs, the farmer can add manure, to improve the fertility of the soil. Ploughing ensures that plenty of organic material is retained in the soil, but above all, it replaces an existing ecosystem with a simplified version containing only man's choice of a limited range of plants.

Soil is not a guaranteed feature of the natural world; it is a finite resource that has taken many thousands of years to form. Today, a worrying aspect of the use of land for agriculture is the rate at which soil is being lost. Many farmers would argue that they have improved their techniques and now produce higher-yielding, better-quality crops. However, their increasing use of pesticides and chemical fertilizers, while ensuring improved crops, hides the fact that both the quality and the quantity of topsoil are being reduced. The land is becoming poorer.

The removal of soil from the land by natural means is known as erosion. It is the greatest cause of soil loss. In Europe, land that is intensively cultivated for crops grown in rows (with bare earth left in between) may lose as much as 100 tonnes of soil per hectare each year. In the USA erosion has meant an end to farming on no fewer than 14 million hectares of agricultural land. Long-term research has shown that many causes of erosion are so ordinary that they go unnoticed until it is too late.

In Britain, removing hedges in order to create larger fields for the larger machines, and to avoid the need for hedgerow maintenance, has left expanses of soil open and exposed to strong winds. After removing the hedgerow the farmer experiences clouds of soil drifting across his land, smothering crops and blocking country lanes.

Another cause of soil erosion are the large, heavy machines used by modern farmers. (There were over 364,000 tractors in England alone in 1985.) These machines compact the soil, making it difficult for rain to penetrate the surface. Instead, the water washes down the slope of the field, taking valuable soil with it. This problem is made worse when tractors are driven down, rather than across, the slope. The wheel tracks form channels along which a large volume of water can run at high speed. Soon a gully may begin to develop, and so erosion will be accelerated. A similar problem is encountered in parts of Africa, where well-worn pathways between villages become so compacted that in the same way they form gullies and erosion begins.

The soil which is washed from the fields must finish up somewhere else. Often it is deposited in natural water courses which then become so clogged up that they cannot function properly.

By cultivating down rather than across the slope the farmer has encouraged erosion and his seed has either been washed away with the soil or buried deep, creating a patchy crop of oilseed rape.

Worldwide, erosion is not the only threat to soil. An increase in the amount of soluble salt contained in the soil is also a major problem. Large quantities of water are naturally held underground, near the earth's surface, in what are known as aquifers. These are often an important source of water for drinking or irrigation. In parts of Britain in the nineteenth century, excessive amounts of underground water were pumped to supply the growing needs of the Industrial Revolution, and this resulted in saline seawater flowing into the aquifers in the rock. Today, too much salt in the soil (salinity) is mainly a problem of arid and semi-arid areas.

Salinity is common where irrigation brings about a rise in the groundwater. This water eventually reaches the surface, evaporates and leaves the salts behind on the surface of the soil. A similar effect results when surface water is required, as in rice cultivation.

In Western Australia, the main cause of salinity of the soil has been the clearance of natural vegetation. The crops introduced in its place need a smaller amount of the water supplied by rainfall. Some of the unneeded rainwater disappears as run-off, but much remains and enters the deeper groundwater systems. Slowly, the groundwater level rises, dissolving salts in the soil, and brings them to the surface. The water then evaporates and the salts are left behind. By 1988 well over 300,000 hectares of land in Western Australia had been made useless for farming through salinity. The problem has been worsening by 10,000 hectares each year.

In northern Somalia over-grazing of land and the resultant loss of vegetation has caused rainwater to run off more rapidly, forming gullies – a dramatic kind of erosion.

Growing energy

Farming is all about energy. The energy of the sun is harnessed by plants in the process of photosynthesis. Animals, in turn, receive this energy when they are fed the crop. Humans then receive some of that energy when they eat the product of the animal – milk or eggs – or consume the animal itself.

Contrast this with our life in Britain where we use tremendous quantities of energy in the form of fuel, to produce our food supply. In the period 1950-70 fuel was cheap, while labour was increasingly expensive. Therefore, along with many Western nations, Britain developed a system of food supply that relies heavily on fuel inputs, particularly oil products and electricity. To supply food to one person in Britain, three times as much fuel is used than the average amount supplied to meet all the needs (cooking, heating, travel, manufacturing) of one person in a developing nation. As world fossil fuel resources are limited, we would do little service to others if we were to encourage them to copy

A valuable fuel being wasted: straw-burning in Britain. The tractor is busy ploughing a fire-break to prevent the flames spreading to nearby woodland.

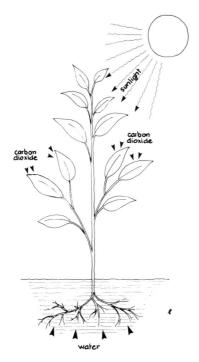

In photosynthesis plants use light, carbon dioxide from the air and water to produce carbohydrates.

us; in many cases, they could not afford to do so.

It is not surprising that an increasing number of nations, including Britain, are looking at methods of producing fuel from farm crops. Britain produces some 12 million tonnes of straw each year. (A field of wheat will yield 4 tonnes of straw per hectare.) Nationally, up to half of this straw has been wasted by farmers who choose the quickest, and cheapest, method for removing it from the field – that is, burning.

Straw has about half the energy, or heating value, of a good sample of coal and rather more than a third of that of fuel oil. It is, therefore, quite an acceptable fuel for firing the domestic boiler of a farmhouse, as farmers are now realizing. Many farmers also require heat for drying purposes, especially for grain, and straw-burning furnaces are being installed to provide the heat source. Some horticulturalists are experimenting with straw-fired boilers for heating greenhouses.

As long ago as 1886 a Californian farmer, George Berry, constructed the first self-propelled combine harvester. It was steam-driven, with two engines powered by one boiler that was fuelled by straw. Had Berry been working with the further knowledge achieved in the twentieth century, he would probably have used straw differently, and in a more efficient way, to produce industrial alcohol for fuelling his machines. And then, like others, he might have found the processing of straw into alcohol too expensive to be worth his while. However, in other countries, different crops have been used quite successfully to produce alcohol, particularly ethanol.

Brazil has a large rural labour force capable of cultivating its well-watered arable lands; but it has very small oil resources. These factors encouraged the government, in 1975, to back a project designed to produce ethanol from sugar-cane. The ethanol is then blended with oil to provide a fuel for cars. Normal car engines will operate quite satisfactorily on this fuel without any modification, but ultimately the government hopes to see a nation of "pure alcohol" car engines. Currently 25% of the nation's cars are fuelled on the pure fuel and the remainder on the mixture. The government believes that this policy will eventually reduce foreign imports of oil by up to 40%. Scientists have suggested that only 3% of available agricultural land in Brazil need be given over to sugar-cane production to make the country entirely self-sufficient in energy.

This project has its critics, who point out that many workers have been displaced from farmland by giant companies. One company alone grows 1700 square km of sugar-cane for alcohol. Cassava (manioc) has proved a suitable alternative to sugar-cane, its particular advantage being that it will grow in most conditions. The next few years may show a move towards growing more cassava instead of sugar-cane, and in fact very large areas of the Amazon forest are being cleared already to make way for this crop. Brazil's pursuit of energy independence could severely harm the environment.

Another country keen to reduce its reliance on oil imports is South Africa, where experts have been looking at the possibility of using vegetable oils. Rudolph Diesel, the German inventor of the engine that bears his name, imagined vegetable oils being used in his engines and believed that this would encourage farmers to grow crops specifically for fuel.

South Africans have also looked at the use as fuel of sunflower oil – more familiar to us as a foodstuff. A one-hectare crop will yield 1.5 tonnes of seed, giving up to 600 litres of oil. Growing and processing requires an input of only 60 litres of fuel and so the crop has a very favourable "energy ratio" of 10:1. The resultant oil has been extensively tested in South African tractors, either in its pure form or blended with diesel oil. The engines have been run for many hundreds of hours with almost no difference in output of power and little or no signs of wear.

In New Zealand an even more unlikely substance is blended with diesel oil. In this country where sheep outnumber people by 20:1, it has been found that tallow, a type of hard fat from the body of the animal, can be used quite successfully in diesel engines.

Sugar-cane being harvested in South America. Increasingly, this crop is used as a source of ethanol for fuel rather than to make sugar.

Waste

Britain generates some 30 million tonnes of waste each year. In other words, each of us throws away several times our own weight in rubbish annually. You will be most familiar with the items that make up the contents of your dustbin (household rubbish), but waste is all around us. You can trace the theme of waste through all the sections of this book. It is important to minimize waste if we are effectively to manage the farming and food resources of our planet.

Differing approaches are seen in the example of the broken-down tractor. In Britain, when a tractor fault develops, the farmer, often with the help of a specialist mechanic, identifies the part that has gone wrong, removes it, and substitutes a new item. The faulty part is discarded. Why? In Britain, and other Western nations, we live in a "throw-away" society where resources are cheaper than labour costs. To fit a new part may take only an hour, whereas to repair the old one would take a day.

A farmer's own rubbish tip illustrates the amount of waste we produce. Such tips can often cause pollution and endanger surrounding habitats.

In developing nations, however, the picture is very different. Here, poor farmers cannot afford to throw away something simply because it breaks down; resources are expensive. On the other hand, labour is cheap, and so the answer is to repair rather than replace – that is, providing the farmer knows how. Lack of education in these countries leads to one of the biggest wastes – waste of manpower.

Failing to use equipment correctly can often lead to waste. For instance, revving a tractor engine may give vent to the driver's impatience, but it will not help to cultivate the field any faster. Instead, the wheels will slip a small amount in every revolution. Such bad driving may cause the driver to waste 10% of his power.

The waste of straw from cereal crops was mentioned on pages 24-25. Straw is classed as an "agricultural residue", as is animal dung (see also page 9 of *Pressures on the Countryside*). The case has been made for using straw as fuel, but, against this, concern has been expressed that removing such waste from the land eventually leads to a reduction in soil fertility. In India, 25% of all the cattle dung produced is burnt as fuel, while in China, 60% of all straw and crop stalks are used for the same purpose. Waste management policy could be changed so that those materials, instead of being used as fuel, would be ploughed into the soil. This would reduce the need for chemical fertilizers (now and in the future), but would it lead also to further reductions in tree cover, as alternative fuel supplies were sought?

Our land, particularly that available for agriculture, is a vital resource. To mismanage it in any way is wasteful, because we are not making efficient use of it. We also mismanage, and therefore waste, the resources of the sea, by over-exploiting them. There can be no justification for ruining fish stocks by excessive fishing (see page 38). The catching of non-target species is another serious problem. Depending on the location, fishermen hunting one particular species may catch a host of others which they do not want, from dolphins,

In targeting shrimps, the fisherman will also catch many other species of sea life that are of no use to him. Known as the by-catch, these are usually thrown back into the sea having died in the meantime.

porpoises and whales to sea turtles, seals and many smaller varieties. Invariably these creatures die as a result of being caught. It is thought that shrimp fishers in the Gulf of Mexico catch and discard up to 20 tonnes of other fish for every one tonne of shrimp. This waste is a pattern repeated in such countries as India, Thailand and Indonesia, where the situation is made worse by factory fleets that come inshore indiscriminately removing large populations of shrimps and depriving local people of their food stocks.

An end to diversity

Where farming has become so intensive that it has left the fields and moved indoors, a whole new range of problems is created. Health and welfare are key concerns when animals are kept in unnatural surroundings.

Thirty years ago a typical British lowland farmer would have carried out a wide range of enterprises. Perhaps the central feature of the farm would have been his dairy herd, grazing the fields in summer and feeding off hay in the winter months. As cows can graze only long grass, they would have left behind ample for a flock of sheep to follow them and graze the field further. In other fields there would have been poultry and pigs.

The farmer was equally diverse in his growing of crops. For cereals, he would grow wheat, barley and oats. Potatoes would be in evidence, as would fields of swedes, turnips and mangolds. The latter, together with kale, provided an important supply of fodder for his farm animals. Most farmhouses would have had a sizeable orchard.

This traditional image of British farming is one that continues to be presented by the media, especially in advertizing, but it is far from reality. Today, the farmer is a specialist, for, as in any other business, it is possible to be

more efficient by concentrating on one aspect of the job; and increased efficiency brings about increased profits.

Numerically, one quarter (25%) of all British farms are still 10 hectares or smaller, while 50% of farms in England and Wales are more than 120 hectares. The significance of the large farms is clearly shown by the fact that the largest 1% of holdings (no more than 2,100 farms) produce 15% of the country's agricultural output.

Specialization inevitably has a major impact on the countryside. The farmer who concentrates on dairy farming, for example, grows mainly grass, as each cow needs 5-6 hectares to graze from. His fields therefore are made up of monocultures of Perennial or Italian Ryegrass, dressed with inorganic nitrogenous fertilizers to enhance growth. Repeated grazing, coupled with excess fertility, almost certainly results in the failure of any wild species of plant in the field (even before the farmer begins to spray with herbicide, see page 17). As a result, grasslands which could once support 20 species of butterfly will now probably support

Some British farmers grow only the variety and quantity of crop that they can guarantee to sell. Peas are one example. Before growing, the farmer makes an agreement with a purchaser. "Farming under contract" means that the buyer determines what is produced on the farm.

Guatemala. With a protein content of 10 per cent maize is a highly valued crop throughout the Americas and parts of Africa. The USA is the world's largest producer of maize.

none. In fact, the Nature Conservancy Council has gone as far as to suggest that if all farms were "totally modernized, about 80% of the birds and 95% of the butterfly species would be lost from farmed landscapes".

The semi-natural grasslands of the Chalk Downs are in sharp contrast. Situated in the south and east of England, they have long been a focus of the naturalist's attention, as they are home for so many species. As chalkland drains rapidly, there is never any build-up of nutrients, and this, coupled with low acidity, allows a wide variety of plants to compete on equal terms. The 19,000 hectares of downland that remained in Dorset in 1934 have, however, been reduced to a meagre 3,000 hectares today. Most of the land has been ploughed, often to be replaced by ryegrass.

In many respects the Prairies of North America have suffered the same fate. Once another species-rich grassland, the prairies have been extensively ploughed, with the subsequent loss of hundreds of herbs and grasses. Now, instead, vast tracts of cultivated land support only one species of crop – usually either wheat, maize or alfalfa. Many farming activities referred to in this book have the effect of reducing diversity. A classic example is Brazil's replacement of tropical rainforests with a monoculture based on cassava (see page 25).

Relying on a single crop can invite disaster. This may come in the form of drought or as excessive rain, either of which results in a sometimes total loss of that year's yield. At a national or global level, relying on only one species is, so to speak, to gamble with the world's food requirements. In 1970 in the USA, 80% of the maize lands were threatened by a fungus; what if such a disaster were actually to happen in the wheat or rice fields? Greater diversity in agriculture would not only provide economic security for the farmer, but also ensure that we the consumers were not left without food.

Water

Fresh water is essential to life and a vital commodity to the farmer, yet the city dweller all too often takes it for granted as something readily obtainable at the turn of the tap, or as a nuisance falling from the sky in bad weather.

Sadly, most of the world's available water is unusable. Over 97% of it is saline, more than 2% is locked in polar ice caps and glaciers, and as little as 0.3% is contained in lakes, rivers and the top half mile (0.8 km) of the earth's crust. Recent estimates suggest that we have access to only 0.01% of the earth's water supply.

This means that about 14,000 cubic km of usable water are available annually. Agriculture remains the largest user, taking some 60% of this. In Britain, rearing a dairy cow, for example, requires 70 litres of water each day. Growing 1 kg of wheat requires 1500 litres, whereas producing a similar quantity of rice needs three times that amount of water, because paddy fields have to be flooded to a depth of 15 cm.

Global water usage.

Irrigation 73%
Industry 22%
Domestic 5%

In Britain we suffer only rarely from major water shortages, and so the farmer's main concern is to ensure that his fields are adequately drained. Much of Britain's farmland relies on drainage systems that have been installed and maintained by successive generations of farmers. Surplus water is removed from the soil by a complex pattern of underground drains, once made of clay tile, now of plastic piping. These flow into a network of ditches surrounding the fields.

The most obvious sign of poorly drained land would probably be its very wet nature. Not only

would this prevent cultivation in all but the driest months (and perhaps make it impossible to use today's heavy machines), but also it would encourage the growth of sedges and rushes in what might otherwise have been good grazing land. Another problem is that water-logged soil takes much longer to warm up, as the energy of the sun has to raise the temperature of the water as well as the soil. A crop sown in soil which then becomes waterlogged will therefore be much slower in beginning its growth cycle.

Plants need oxygen which they take from water in the soil, and yet excessive amounts of water in the soil displace the air supply and prevent aeration, so that vital oxygen supplies are not replenished. In addition, a lack of oxygen in the soil can bring about the production of methane and hydrogen sulphide, both of which are toxic to plant roots. Finally, too much water in the soil will inhibit the development of micro-organic life-forms, and slow down the natural process of decomposition, causing a loss of soil fertility and a build-up in acidity.

Paradoxically, many carefully drained fields then receive their own artificial supply of water, through a pipe ending in a trough. One reason for this is that studies of animal behaviour have shown that a dairy cow will not walk more than 250 metres to obtain the water she needs to maintain her milk yield. On the other hand, root crops such as potatoes require irrigation to ensure maximum yield. So a farmer frequently obtains an abstraction licence which permits him to pump water from a nearby river or large stream.

Field drains.

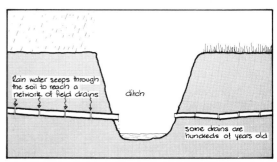

Rain water seeps through the soil to reach a network of field drains

ditch

some drains are hundreds of years old

Irrigation is carried out on 15% of the world's croplands, and is essential for the production of 30% of our food. In general, the methods used are quite wasteful of water, and consequently more efficient methods are being examined. Trickle irrigation, for instance, involves constructing a network of pipes to conduct water directly to individual plants.

Trees can be grown in desert regions, as the Israelis have shown in the Negev, where each tree has its own specially constructed water catchment area. The principles of this method, known as "water harvesting", have been studied and applied in an Oxfam project in Burkina Faso. The rapidly expanding population of this small African nation put heavy pressures on crop growers in their effort to obtain more food. Lengthy fallow periods which once rested the soil and allowed it to recover have been abandoned. The soil has been reduced in quality and often eroded away. The Oxfam project built 40-cm-high rock walls – often for several hundred metres – along the contours of the fields. These *diguettes*, as they are known, capture water that might otherwise have run off across the hard, sun-dried earth and been lost. They are particularly valuable in drought years, when rainfall on its own would be insufficient to produce satisfactory crops.

In Burkina Faso local communities have been organized to build simple rock walls which "harvest" any rainwater.

Irrigation is a means of ensuring that crops grow in previously unused land – in this case in Ethiopia. The trees being watered will form a windbreak once they grow larger.

To ensure a plentiful crop of potatoes, the British farmer must keep his field well watered in dry weather. Irrigation (watering) relies on a good natural supply of unpolluted water.

Too much milk

Apart from the climate, two major factors shape the environment of lowland Britain – diet and economics. In a year, the average Briton eats 7 kg of cheese and 5.4 kg of butter as well as consuming (in one form or another) 112 kg of milk (about 25 gallons). To meet the demands of this "dairy produce diet", lowland dairy farmers produce some 34 million litres of milk each day for collection by the Milk Marketing Board.

Milk production actually exceeds demand. Normally, such an excess of a product would bring about a price reduction followed by a reduced supply, and the producer or manufacturer would suffer a loss. However, the business of dairy-farming has remained profitable because, instead of allowing prices to fall, the government-supported Milk Marketing Board fixes a stable, often artificially high, price for milk. So the government's economic policy, in favouring dairy farms, shapes our countryside.

The seemingly endless market for milk ensured that, in the period 1960-82, the average size of a dairy herd in the UK rose from 37 to 58

By using ample dressings of fertilizer, a farmer can harvest several crops of fodder from one field of grass between May and September. British farmers mow their grass and then collect it with a forage harvester. It is stored as silage and fed to cattle in winter.

cows. Through improvements in efficiency and husbandry, the average milk yield per cow rose from 3500 litres to 4800 litres per year. Total milk production in this period increased, even though the number of dairy farmers decreased from 180,000 to 59,000.

As there was a ready market for his milk, the dairy farmer was encouraged to expand his business and, as we see from the average herd size, farms became much larger. Medium-sized herds (100 cows or fewer) are frequently run as one "unit" – that is, all the animals are kept, and moved, together. Many cattle kept in a small area would soon destroy the structure of the soil beneath their hooves. They would wear out the grass sward and would need to be frequently moved to another field to find enough grazing. To avoid these problems, modern dairy farmers have made their fields bigger.

During the winter, cattle have to be given fodder grown during the summer months. Traditionally this has been hay, but more recently it has tended to be silage. Scientists have helped the farmer by developing highly productive, quick-growing strains of grass that respond well to the range of chemical fertilizers they can also offer him. Beginning in late May, the same field can yield three crops – or "cuts" – of silage before the end of the summer.

In his continuing search for efficiency and maximum profits from milk, the farmer has made other changes. As well as building a large "cubicle house" for his growing herd to shelter in, he has probably installed a "parlour", where a more efficient milking system can be operated. If he has added to this a covered collecting yard for the cattle, a silage barn to replace the traditional hay barn, plus a slurry tank, or lagoon, to contain the animal waste, his dairy unit may well resemble a factory complex.

There has been a dramatic turn of fortunes, however, for the ambitious and successful British dairy farmer. In 1984, in an attempt to regulate the surplus of milk, the European Economic Community introduced a system which determines the maximum amount of milk that any one farm can produce in a year. This figure, given in litres, is known as the "milk quota". Many farmers are being forced to

In Britain, dairy cows must be housed indoors in winter. The dairy, collecting yard, cubicle house, silage barn and slurry lagoon cover a large area. Here British Friesians are being fed silage in the cubicle house.

reduce their milk output and, as a result, high-yielding grassland is being replaced by fields growing crops ranging from wheat for animal feed to evening primrose for the pharmaceutical industry. Some farmers have stopped producing milk altogether and have entered the property market, selling spare fields for building, or applying for planning permission to turn now redundant farm buildings into "desirable rural dwellings".

Living in a society so dominated by milk and its products, we may find it hard to believe that milk is not thought of as equally important in the rest of the world. Britain is the second-largest milk-drinker in Europe – Ireland being the largest. By contrast, in the greater part of Asia and much of Africa few adults consume milk – often because of allergies or an intolerance of lactose. About 10% of the protein in the Indian diet comes from milk, but, since milk production in India is limited by a shortage of cattle fodder, only the richer people living in the cities can get a regular supply.

Perhaps the most significant difference between Britain and the developing world is the way in which we have established herds of healthy cattle. It is very unusual to see a sick animal in this country, and yet it has been estimated that, globally, more than 50 million cattle and buffalo are killed each year by disease and parasites.

In rural India farmers take their milk to a collection centre every morning.

Too much land?

Today, as you read this, one in ten people in the world will not eat enough food to keep healthy, let alone to maintain their body weight. Yet we are producing too much food. This is a major issue facing not only the European Economic Community, of which Britain is a member, but also the USA.

In the developed world, the traditional main aim of the agricultural industry has been to produce as much food as possible. Agricultural scientists have devoted their attentions to increasing yields on good land and to finding ways of bringing poorer-quality land to acceptable levels of production.

The success of their efforts is most apparent in the increased yields of cereal grains. In 1950 the average UK wheat yield was 3.5 tonnes per hectare, but this has now risen to over 6 tonnes per hectare. Indeed, it would be possible today to grow a crop with an annual yield of over 15 tonnes per hectare – but farmers would find it impracticable to do so (see pages 14-15, Chemical fertilizers).

One of the major roles of the Ministry of Agriculture, Fisheries and Food (MAFF) has been to give grants to farmers who wished to improve land that was too wet. In the period 1970-80 the area of land subject to grant-aided drainage quadrupled to 100,000 hectares per year, and this spelt disaster for birds breeding and wintering in the wetlands.

During that decade when British farmers brought more and more land into food production, the number of people in the country increased by only 500,000; there was no rapidly increasing population to be fed. Perhaps you would guess that the new farmland was meant to replace other areas lost to urban development? But, in fact, over the same period the amount of agricultural land lost to the building industry remained steady at around 16,000 hectares per year. This is even decreasing and is now about 13,000 hectares per year. If all the land lost had been wheatland, then surplus grain stocks might have been reduced by some 70,000 tonnes annually. Agriculturalists calculate this to be not far from the annual increase in yields in recent years, brought about by improved technology. In other words, land loss is balanced by increased efficiency. The National Farmers' Union has also estimated that if 700,000 hectares of British farmland were removed from agricultural production between 1986 and 1990 there would be no adverse effect on food production.

Slowly but surely, farmers are beginning to interpret the statistics. No longer do they need to plan for expansion. They must rather adjust their approach to farming if they wish to continue as a profitable business. Conservationists are looking on keenly, as the environment stands to gain in many ways.

When too much grain is produced the price will slump and farmers make no profit. To prevent this, agencies intervene and surplus grain in Britain is purchased with money from the EEC and put into an Intervention Store.

Terraced fields in Nepal allow for the maximum amount of land to be farmed.

A farmer might decide to be less intensive in his methods so as to reduce his outputs, particularly of grain and milk. He would then want to reduce his input in the same proportion, and this would almost certainly lead to a reduction in the use of very high-cost items, such as pesticides and fertilizers.

Alternatively, a farmer might deliberately leave land uncultivated for a specified number of years; this is known as "set-aside". He would receive a government grant to offset his reduced revenue, and the system could operate in three different ways. The first of these, field set-aside, would require whole fields to be taken out of production for at least a year at a time. The value of this to wildlife is questionable. The second way, headland set-aside, would involve leaving uncultivated a strip of, say, 10 metres around the edge of the field. Such strips adjacent to hedges or ponds would rapidly be colonized by existing populations of birds, small mammals and insects and could be of tremendous value. The third way, whole farm set-aside, is the most drastic and could result in major wildlife havens. It is the least likely of the three schemes to be adopted, however. Experimental field set-aside began in West Germany in the autumn of 1986, and in 1987 the United States' Government's set-aside programme aimed to take 15% of farmers' growing area out of production.

Set-aside would not be without its problems, and many farmers are concerned that, rather than developing conservation areas, this policy would lead to the development of weed-infested areas, harbouring soil pests and diseases which are currently kept in check by methods of cultivation. Perhaps there is a need to re-educate some farmers, to help them see that plants they have tried to get rid of can be seen as wild flowers, not weeds.

However, agricultural scientists may have highlighted an even greater problem for those advocating set-aside. Growing crops uses large quantities of nitrogen from the soil. In soil without a growing crop there will be unused, surplus nitrogen, and this will be leached out of the soil and into water-courses, probably leading to high levels of water pollution. It will be ironic if farmers, the very people who cause water-course pollution by spreading nitrogenous fertilizer, use this argument to prevent set-aside.

In England and Wales some 37 per cent of the land is given over to arable farming. Is this too much? Globally, we cultivate only some 11 per cent of the ice-free land surface – about 1.5 thousand million hectares. This is not enough to sustain a rapidly growing world population, and yet much of the remainder is unsuitable for growing crops as it suffers from drought (true of a massive 44% of land in Africa), or waterlogging, or shallow soils, or excessively cold conditions. While millions starve, the economy of the developed nations dictates that we reduce the amount of land we cultivate.

Whilst fertile land in Britain is taken out of use for food production, fragile areas such as this in Ethiopia are developed for agricultural purposes.

Food from wildlife

In Britain today you will only rarely find wildlife for sale as food. Some specialist shops sell rabbit or game birds such as pheasant or partridge, but the latter have usually been reared in captivity and then released into the wild as game for sportsmen. (See the book on *Hunting, Shooting and Fishing*, also in this series.)

Deer farming has become well-established in this country in the last ten years and there are now some 200 commercial deer farms. Despite the occasional introduction of wild stock, the 10,000 hinds kept for breeding purposes are clearly domesticated animals. British deer farming therefore contrasts sharply with the man/animal relationship in Lapland between the people and the reindeer. Although the economy of the Laplanders has developed around this single species, they have not domesticated it. The reindeer remain wild, and the people follow the migrations of the animals, rather than the reindeers' way of life being controlled by the people.

In the countries of southern Africa, careful management has enabled cattle farmers to encourage other species alongside their domesticated cattle. If they were to increase the numbers of cattle in the *bushveld*, this would

Some British shops still specialize in the sale of game, although many of their products were reared to release into the wild.

Deer farming is becoming increasingly popular in Britain, as it can make use of poorer land and there is a ready market for venison in shops and restaurants.

result in over-grazing, with disastrous consequences for the future of the grassland. However, if they artificially increase the numbers of wild ungulates – for example, springbok – there is no danger of over-grazing, since these animals browse from the trees and bushes and thus utilize a different food supply. Only a limited amount of management is necessary, and by killing a number of these wild animals each year the farmer is able to increase the supply of meat without any major farming input.

A recent experiment in Mozambique, centred on the Zambesi Wildlife Utilization Area, has shown that where there is deliberate cropping of wild animals in order to supply meat, there is also a considerable reduction in poaching. This approach has not only provided food for the local population and been of economic benefit, but has also protected wildlife by preventing the excessive slaughter of any one species.

Farm meat tends to be expensive and, consequently, where a local population is poor and the wildlife abundant, wild animal meat is a major source of protein in the diet. In Botswana, for example, over 2 million spring hares are killed by hunters each year. To us, this may seem an unacceptable slaughter of wildlife. However, to obtain the same quantity of meat from cattle, it would be necessary to raise and slaughter 20,000 beasts annually. Setting up enough cattle farms to achieve this in Botswana, even if it were feasible, could well result in habitat destruction on such a scale that the hare population would be drastically reduced anyway. Studies of the diet of cattle-rearing tribesmen in Botswana have shown that they still obtain 80% of their meat from wildlife, and only 20% from their own livestock.

The wild animals that provide the most plentiful supplies of food are often the smaller creatures, many of them rodents. In Nigeria, attempts are being made to domesticate the African giant rat and the grass-cutter rat, whilst in South America it has been realized that the capybara – the world's largest rodent – is a valuable source of meat.

Rodents have a much higher reproductive rate than most other animals and so it is possible to "harvest" them in large numbers and still sustain the yield. A capybara, for example, will produce well over thirty offspring in its lifetime. Nonetheless, in Venezuela, this animal is being displaced by "traditional" farming methods. The grassland, or savannah, is turned over to cattle that will produce only ten calves over a similar period. If you compare the amount of land required to support a population of capybara with the grazing needed for cattle, it becomes apparent that the capybara produces a larger quantity of meat from a given area. This appears to be a case of man not appreciating the value of the wildlife around him, but would you eat capybara? Perhaps not. In neighbouring Peru, many people eat guinea pig.

The kangaroo in Australia is thought to be the victim of the world's biggest commercial exploitation of land-based wildlife. Farmers can point to the kangaroo, particularly the big red and grey, as a pest which competes directly with their own livestock for grassland. Such a pest needs to be controlled. Those who vehemently oppose the annual killing of over 2 million of

The kangaroo can be a lucrative crop; its skin is even used to make sports footwear. The conservation organization Greenpeace is campaigning against this.

these animals argue that it is done not as pest control but for personal financial gain and the macabre pleasure of kangaroo hunting. In an attempt to discourage persecution of these animals, the Greenpeace organization has been highlighting the fact that kangaroo hides are sold for use in footwear such as trainers.

One note of caution: if we no longer rely on a particular animal species for our food, that animal does not stop being important. Each living creature has its role to play in maintaining a balanced ecosystem. It is on that balance that our future world depends.

Harvesting the sea

Whereas we have largely domesticated the *animals* which we use for food, we are still, generally speaking, hunters of wildlife when it comes to harvesting the living resources of the sea. Attempts at fish farming are small-scale and more appropriate to fresh water.

To prevent over-fishing, certain controls have been placed on fishermen. Rules about nets, for example, say that the mesh size must be large enough for smaller – and younger – fish to escape, while only the largest ones are caught. But many of the regulations have been too few, too late and weakly imposed.

In fact, local fishermen are usually aware that their livelihood depends on future generations of fish and so it is not in their financial interest to catch young stock. By contrast, fishermen working for large competitive companies, on vessels capable of travelling long distances and of staying at sea for weeks rather than days, have become opportunists, obtaining a catch wherever they can. It is hard to accept the warnings of scientists about over-fishing when the only way that you can recover the capital investment in your boats is to put to sea and catch fish to sell. It is difficult to stay in port when you know that there is a demand for any

British fishing ports are no longer bustling with activity; many fishing vessels now lie idle and the fishermen are unemployed. Did they bring this upon themselves?

fish that you can catch and that if you don't catch them, others will. Over-exploitation of fish stocks has been almost inevitable.

On the Dogger Bank, off the English coast to the east of Great Yarmouth, the annual herring catch fell 30-fold over just 15 years, until, in 1966, only 10,000 tonnes were caught. But that was just one fishery. In more northerly waters the catch became so low that fishing was stopped, and in 1977 a total ban was implemented on herring fishing throughout the North Sea. This ban lasted for 6 years. Similar stories about reductions in the catch can be told about other species, such as cod and haddock.

WORLD FISHERIES

Examples of major exploitation

fishery	% of potential catch
North West Pacific	100
North East Atlantic	90
East Central Atlantic	70
West Central Pacific	66
North West Atlantic	55
Eastern Pacific	50

The % figure represents the percentage currently caught annually of the total sustainable catch.

It is thought that about 25 of the world's most valuable fisheries are seriously depleted, while many more have suffered so extensively at the hands of the uncoordinated international fishing industry that they are unlikely to recover. The end-result of this over-exploitation is that today, at best, the annual world catch of fish is 25 per cent lower than it might have been if man had made sensible use of this enormous natural source of food.

An example of the ruination of a fish stock is that of the anchoveta fishery in Peru and Northern Chile. Here, once again, scientists one of the group of sea creatures called crustaceans. Countries such as Madagascar, Pakistan and Panama export large quantities, earning vital money from overseas. Until a generation ago, fresh shrimps were a common sight on market stalls in Britain, but now they have virtually disappeared from our waters, as have shellfish, as a result mainly of the industrial and domestic pollution of coastlines and estuaries. (See the cover illustration of Swansea Bay.) Throughout Asia and Africa the destruction of mangrove swamps has removed habitats vital to the life cycle of the shrimp. Other creatures can also be affected. In the USA, for example, disruption of estuarine habitats, through either development or pollution, has made over 25,000 square km unsuitable for shellfishing.

Of course, we do not get all the fish we eat from the large sea-fishing industry. Freshwater rivers and lakes also provide major supplies of fish. Like many coastal areas in developing nations, rivers and lakes are fished by individuals or small groups who try to supply their own food needs and, if possible, earn a living by selling what they catch as well. At least 25 per cent of the world's catch of fish (from sea and fresh water), and over 40 per cent of that used for human consumption, comes from such people. At the mercy of nature's forces and on the receiving end of many man-made disasters, they are hindered by the low level of their technology. Fisherfolk are some of the world's poorest people.

A small catch for some fishermen in Sri Lanka.

were able to warn that fishing could not continue at present rates. In spite of their warnings, though, by 1970, 1500 fishing vessels were making a daily catch of 100,000 tonnes. Two years later that figure had risen to 180,000 tonnes per day. Such a large catch must have included most of the spawnings of the previous two years. Once the breeding stock was gone, the industry collapsed.

As well as fish, a variety of other food sources, from seaweed to whalemeat, is provided by the oceans of the world. The world's most valuable wild animal is the shrimp,

Fish ponds such as these in Sarawak, Malaysia, here being emptied, provide country people with a ready source of protein that would otherwise be lacking in their diet.

Aid to the farmer

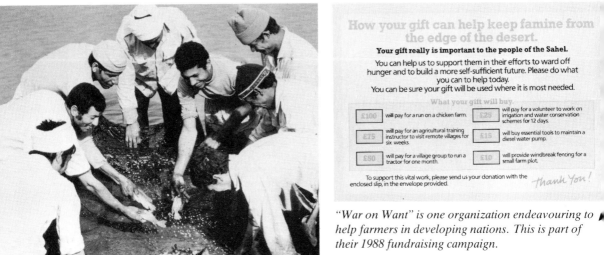

"War on Want" is one organization endeavouring to help farmers in developing nations. This is part of their 1988 fundraising campaign.

Organizations such as ▲ the World Bank Group provide financial aid to farmers. Here money has been provided to introduce Chinese freshwater fish farming technology to an Egyptian fish farm.

The Royal Agricultural Society of England stages an ▶ annual show so that farmers can gain up-to-date information about the farming industry.

◀ British farmers can apply for a wide range of grants to improve the environment of their farm for wildlife. Creating ponds and tree planting are two of the most popular reasons for grant aid.

Many farmers now realize that good farming does not ➤ have to exclude many plants that grow naturally in the area. The Farming and Wildlife Advisory Group employs Countryside Advisers who can help farmers integrate wildlife into the farmscape.

◀ In Britain the Ministry of Agriculture, Fisheries and Food (MAFF) employs staff to visit farmers and give them advice.

Britain is largely free of cattle disease, but overseas ➤ livestock are attacked by a wide range of diseases which result in losses in productivity. Before a vaccination programme such as this in southern Sudan can take place, the people must be educated by aid workers into understanding the value of animal health.

Throughout the world farmers gain up-to-the-minute ▲ advice via radio (and in some countries TV). Here farmers in Pakistan listen to a daily broadcast prepared by their College of Agriculture.

41

What can I do to help?

This book has concerned itself with two closely related issues: food and farming on the one hand, conservation on the other. I have added a third dimension by looking at these issues from not only a British, but also a global point of view. For you as an individual to help in any way at all probably seems a daunting task.

Hew Watt, a well-known British farmer and broadcaster, said to a conference of the Farming and Wildlife Advisory Group (FWAG) in 1986:

"The great problem that has bedevilled civilization since its creation is: how should wealth be created and distributed? It is at the root of all economic and social affairs. For too long we have been obsessed with the excitement of new technical developments and forgotten

Grain being delivered to a Health Centre in Uganda. In the long term it is more important to give seed grain than food.

that it is people and their living on this earth that matters. It is people, not machines, that we should be worrying about."

I believe it was such a concern for people that made "Band Aid" and, subsequently, "Sport Aid" such a success. News reports had made us all very conscious of the plight of the starving people in Africa. Bob Geldof's popularity and direct approach were sufficient to make many of

Mother and child waiting for food at a UNICEF relief station. Famine is, however, not just a twentieth-century phenomenon.

Farmers will be encouraged to retain such important wildlife habitats as this, a refuge from the cultivated land, if they know that volunteer conservationists, such as the British Trust for Conservation Volunteers, will come to carry out maintenance work.

us dig deep into our pockets, and his fund-raising campaigns became the most successful of all time.

Geldof realized that if the problem was not to be repeated, the results of his efforts must operate in two ways. Firstly, the immediate problem of starvation must be overcome; people who are ill through lack of food cannot help themselves. Secondly, and more importantly for its long-term effects, the money raised must be channelled into activities that would help the people produce their own food in the future. Aid is not simply about making a problem better, but about ensuring, as far as we can, that it does not occur again.

Of course, it is relatively easy to dip in our pockets, and then carry on living just as before. If it was pointed out to us, however, that our favourite beefburger was made from the meat of cattle that grazed on pastures created by destroying rainforests, would we be prepared to give up eating them, as a mark of our protest against that destruction?

Western demand for tobacco has encouraged many small farmers in developing nations to grow this cash crop instead of food. In countries as far apart as Kenya and Nepal the removal of surrounding trees to provide wood for curing the tobacco has resulted in major soil loss and damage. Knowing this, would we give up smoking, or even discourage the multi-national tobacco companies from promoting their product?

A supermarket manager will tell you that the British housewife prefers blemish-free, colourful, clean and even-sized fruit and vegetables. To obtain these, the farmer must place many controls on his crops. He may seek new varieties of plant and gear his farming techniques to ensure that he meets the supermarket requirements. Farming and food production are shaped by the consumer's demands.

What *can* you do to help, then? First of all, make quite sure that you understand the connection between the food you eat and the means by which it is grown. Secondly, make up your own mind as to whether or not the farming processes involved are environmentally acceptable, and whether the conservation aspects are being considered sufficiently. Finally, remember that you, as a shopper, have very real power. You can choose whether to buy the food that is displayed, or, after careful thought about the way the farmer has produced it, you can leave it there on the shelf!

43

Glossary

aeration	Keeping sufficient air in the soil. Between the solid particles of soil are spaces (pores) which are filled with air and water. The plant roots use up the oxygen in the air and this must be replaced; if it is not, carbon dioxide may build up to such an extent that it poisons the plant.
botanist	Someone who specializes in the study of plants.
bushveld	The open grassland areas of South Africa; *veld* is an Afrikaans word.
cash crop	A crop grown to generate profit for the individual or the producer country through export.
cropping	The cultivation and subsequent harvesting of an agricultural plant. (The term can also apply to animals.)
crop rotation	A system of farming by which different crops are grown on the same land in a carefully planned sequence.
cultivar	A *culti*vated *vari*ety of a wild species of plant or animal that has been specially developed to emphasize certain characteristics.
developing countries	Those countries of Africa, Asia and South America that are, as yet, in economical terms only poorly developed; sometimes the term *Third World* is used, whilst in more recent years the distinction between *North* and *South* has been made. The North is all those nations above the dotted line shown on the world map on the front cover of this book, the South, or Third World, all those below the line.
erosion	The wearing away of land surfaces (rocks and soil) by various natural elements such as water or wind in conjunction with ice, sun and sand. Human beings may also cause the same effects as natural erosion.
indigenous	Describes a plant or animal, including humans, that lives naturally in an area and has not been introduced.
lactose	Also known as "milk sugar", it is a white crystalline disaccharide which occurs in milk.
larva (plural **larvae**)	Most advanced insects go through a four-stage life cycle. Beginning as an egg, they hatch into a larva (eg grub or caterpillar), change to a *pupa* and finally emerge in adult form.
North/South	see *Developing countries* above.
organic material	Usually, plant material that will decompose in the soil to form humus. Soil is basically made up of two components, the loose rock and mineral fragments from which it is derived and the remains of plants that have previously grown there, or been brought there by the farmer.
photosynthesis	The process in which the chlorophyll contained in green plants captures light energy and uses it to build simple raw materials (carbon, hydrogen and oxygen) into complex, energy-storing materials called carbohydrates.
pollination	The conveying of pollen from the male part of the flower to the female part. Pollen may blow on the wind, be transferred by insects or even by man. The process results in fertilization.
pupa (plural **pupae**)	As many insects develop they change from being a *larva* to a pupa; this is a non-mobile stage when many internal changes will occur before the insect emerges as an adult.
rhizome	A root-like stem that grows horizontally through the ground and sprouts both shoots and roots.
sub-Sahara	The large area of semi-desert and dry grassland that stretches across Africa to the south of the Sahara Desert.
Third World	see *developing countries* above.
tractor power	The power of a tractor engine is measured in the SI unit *watt*. One watt is equal to one joule per second. One megawatt = one million watts.
ungulates	Hoofed mammals.

Useful addresses

The following organizations provide a range of resource material that will provide useful information for you; not all of this material is free. A number of the organizations listed may have regional offices that will be able to help you. Please ensure that you always enclose an A4 size stamped addressed envelope with your enquiry.

National bodies

Royal Agricultural Society of
  England
(British Food and Farming),
35, Belgrave Square,
London, SW1X 8QN

The National Farmers' Union,
Farming Information Centre,
Agriculture House,
Knightsbridge,
London, SW1X 7NJ

The Country Landowners'
  Association,
16, Belgrave Square,
London, SW1X 8PQ

Nature Conservancy Council,
Publications Dept,
Northminster House,
Peterborough, PE1 1UA

Ministry of Agriculture, Fisheries
  & Food,
(Publications),
Lion House,
Willowburn Trading Estate,
Alnwick,
Northumberland

Representatives of the industry

Apple and Pear Development
  Council,
Union House,
The Pantiles,
Tunbridge Wells,
Kent, TN4 8HF

British Agrochemicals
  Association,
4, Lincoln Court,
Lincoln Road,
Peterborough, PE1 2RP

British Farm Produce Council,
417, Market Towers,
New Covent Garden Market,
1, Nine Elms Lane,
London, SW8 5NQ

British Sugar Bureau,
140, Park Lane,
Londokn, W1Y 3AA

British Egg Industry Council,
Farming Information Centre,
Agriculture House,
Knightsbridge,
London, SW1X 7NJ

Butter Information Council,
Tubs Hill House,
London Road,
Sevenoaks,
Kent, TN13 1BL

Fertilizer Manufacturers'
  Association,
Greenhill House,
90-93, Cowcross Street,
London, EC1M 6BH

Flour Advisory Bureau,
21, Arlington Street,
London, SW1A 1RN

Forestry Commission,
231, Corstophine Road,
Edinburgh,
EH12 7AT

Fresh Fruit & Vegetable
Information Bureau,
Bury House,
126-128, Cromwell Road,
London, SW7 4ET

Meat and Livestock Commission,
P.O. Box 44,
Queensway House,
Bletchley,
Milton Keynes,
Bucks, MK2 2EF

Milk Marketing Board,
Thames Ditton,
Surrey, KT7 0EL

National Dairy Council,
Education Dept,
5-7, John Princes Street,
London, W1M 0AP

Potato Marketing Board,
50, Hans Crescent,
Knightsbridge,
London, SW1 0NB

Sea Fish Industry Authority,
142-144, Cromwell Road,
London, SW7

Various

Association of Agriculture,
Victoria Chambers,
16/20 Strutton Ground,
London, SW1P 2HP

Centre for World Development
  Education,
Regent's College,
Inner Circle,
Regent's Park,
London, NW1 4NS

International Centre for
  Conservation Education,
Greenfield House,
Guiting Power,
Cheltenham,
Glos, GL54 5TZ

Royal Society for the Protection
  of Birds,
The Lodge,
Sandy,
Bedfordshire, SG19 2DL

Aid organizations
OXFAM,
Education Dept,
274 Banbury Road,
Oxford, OX2 7DZ

The Catholic Fund for Overseas
    Development,
2 Garden Close,
Stockwell Road,
London, SW9 9TY

War on Want,
37-39, Great Guildford Street,
London, SE1 0ES

Resources list

Agriculture, Keith Bowman, Macdonald and Co, 1985
Disappearing Rainforest, Robert Prosser, Dryad Press, 1987
The Encroaching Desert, Norman Farmer, Dryad Press, 1989
Energy, Power Sources and Electricity, Philip Neal, Dryad Press, 1989
Finding out about Modern Farming, Hobsons Ltd, 1986
Food and Farming Resource Pack, Royal Agricultural Society of England, 1988
Pressures on the Countryside, Derrick Golland, Dryad Press, 1986
Science for Survival – Plants and Rainforests in the Classroom, Adam Cade,
    Richmond Publishing Co Ltd, 1986
Sudan: the roots of famine, Nick Cater, Oxfam, 1986
Time for Trees, Joy Palmer, Dryad Press, 1986
War on Waste, Joy Palmer, Dryad Press, 1988
The World's Water, Joy Palmer, Dryad Press, 1987

Index